Cut the Loss

Weasel

Cut the Loss
Weasel

© 2019 Weasel
Cover image by Tabaxitaxi

Weasel Press
Manvel, TX
www.weaselpress.com

https://degenerateweasel.weebly.com

ISBN-13: 978-1-948712-43-9

Printed in the U.S.A.

ALL RIGHTS RESERVED. This book contains material protected under International and Federal Copyright Laws and Treaties. Any unauthorized reprint or use of this material is prohibited. No part of this book, or use of characters in this book, may be reproduced or transmitted in any form or by any means, electronic or mechanical, including photocopying, recording, or by any information storage and retrieval system without expressed written permission from the author / publisher, except for review and educational purposes.

Cut The Loss is a relationship with vulnerability and heartwords. Weasel has written a collection of touch, broken tongues, and compassion. A true breath of words ala beat poet of our generation.
—Edward Vidaurre, 2018-2019 McAllen, TX Poet Laureate, author of *JAZzHOUSE* and *I Took My Barrio On A Road Trip*

Talented poets have the ability to pack a lot of power into their images and metaphors. Weasel Patterson has this talent, a natural gift which cannot be taught, unlike metrics and form. The poetry in his new collection bristles with this self-same powerful energy and intensity, a riveting reading experience not for the faint-hearted —and not to be missed.
—Thomas White, author of *Ghostly Pornographers*

In this poetry of polyamory and possible psychosis, Weasel Patterson transforms the mundane elements of the writing life (coffee, cigarettes, personal pain, attractive addictions, lost and living love) into truly memorable moments of dark insight. Taking Ferlinghetti's form, summoning the spirits of other Gonzo Beats (Ginsburg, Hunter S), Crowley's mythological masters (Pan, Baphomet) and his own raw experience (outdoor blowjobs, storms, 1st sexual encounters literally in the closet), Weasel turns this "seance of bad choices" into "a manual (on how) to be human". He shows himself as a man who lives by "jamming forks in outlets", dodging "ghosts throwing dildos", and ultimately a soul who cannot be constrained in one love ("little fox") or contained by bourgeois social propriety. Weasel's vibrant and important work offers a raw honesty that makes most of the rest of so-called cutting edge artists seem

like dull butter knives in comparison.
—PoetKen Jones, author of *Life Expectancy,* and *Mr. Karma*

With unflinching imagery and unvarnished emotions, the poet sets us on a journey to discover the "art of detachment" from our relationships (gay or straight), our pasts, our reality, our suicidal ideations, our fear of the inexorability of death, and our terror of the inevitability of life.

As we travel, the poet invites us to linger with his Muses, to observe as he challenges, converses, argues and accepts the truths they offer. Ginsberg questions, "What good is enlightenment when you have never felt fulfilled?" Kerouac reassures, "it's just a giant road everything in front and all that's left behind forgotten." Bukowski shouts, "are the fires of madness worth the prayer to lessen the pain?" We move on with the taunting voice of Selby in our ear, "life is a dream fading.
—LuLynne Streeter, author of *Frozen Lives*, and editor of Hollering Woman Press

Contents

the sound inside	1

The Muses

allen ginsberg meditates while i eat breakfast	5
hunter s. thompson aims his pistol at me	7
bukowski's ghost watches me fuck from the corner	9
i used a ouija board to talk to kerouac	10
hubert selby jr. drinks coffee in my kitchen	12

I

i talk in broken tongues	17
love is not a synonym for monogamy	18
my notebook is falling apart	19
depression devours me from the inside	21
the wife/the faggot	23
he says he knows why i smoke	25
i fuckin' hate knowin' a storm is comin'	27
i met apollo at a crossroad in texas	28
the art of attachment	30
the coffee at ihop sucks	32
i met him in the woods for a quick blow-n-go	33
i have trouble staying in the present	34
the fire burns fierce this morning	36
the gas station of dull disdain	38

II

when i heard you turned wishes into bombs	43
the first night	44
when we got married	45
i paint disasters when you're not around	47
love ain't no fuckin' mercy	48
i return to you, love	50
i could see the anger bubble in your belly	51
you are scrubbing the scuff-marks off the wall	53
i don't get drunk	55

i never wanted to write our break-up poem	57
i dropped him off at the greyhound	59
the future is another ditch, beginning at dirt	61
i took your spot on the bed	63

III

a house of broken ghosts	67
the clown sits on my wall	68
i wrote my suicide note on a napkin	69
i ain't no prayin' man	71
afterglow on a desk stained with coffee	73
morning coffee at the gas station	74
he asked me to eat his ass	76
the boss lost to the carnage of a drunk driver	78
hipnos	79
everytime i call	80

IV

the grogginess of your voice	83
i like that you call me star	84
my tongue longs for the taste of you	85
i never understood the appeal of fucking in a shower	86
i think about your touch on the coldest nights	88
it's been months since i've seen you	90
you wear me out	91
i never thought it'd be cold in april	92
i've never been blown in a graveyard	93
love is a gospel, and i'm still learning	95
your heart is just the chatter of your body	97
i drove with aphrodite on i-10	99
the first time you get blown at disney	101
eros makes reservations	104
a past fragmented	107

V

punk rock taught me that life is a moment	111
the ghost in my house keeps throwing dildos at me	112

my dating profile	114
we all know goofy fucks	117
goofy walks into a club	118
pan's flute plays in disarray	119
i met satan on grindr	121
everyone is so afraid of demons	123
the americana	124
compassion is often rough	126
when my lights go out	128
exit	131

Introduction

This collection is tough. Tough writing. Tough thinking. And overall bruised to hell. I'm not blowin' smoke up my own ass neither. The pages that follow are my way of processing some heavy shit. Poetry is that for me, a method of working through trauma and mental abuse. A way to understand and to cope. Poetry is healing.

Cut the Loss is all about letting go of your attachments; about realizing when your story is becoming unhealthy and needs a deep edit. My story is a whole mess of confusion, haunted by experiences of emotional abuse, suicidal ideation, and love. And I need a lotta love.

I'm polyamorous. If you're unfamiliar with that term, it means I love more than one individual, and that I practice ethical non-monogamy. I ain't here to debate the ethics of multiple relationships, you can email me later and I'll decide if I really want to spend that energy. I firmly believe that you can love two people (or more) equally. I have a husband, and I have a boyfriend. I love the fuck out of both of them, and I've dedicated a section for each.

In the case of my husband, A, I don't hate him. I've never stopped loving him. But there are things I can't fully process (or forgive). His section will speak on its own.

My mental health is in disarray, but I'm workin' on it. Healing is a slow process and I'm still at the start of that art. But that's all life, ain't it?

Before closing the book, thank the Muses on your way out. Otherwise they'll bother you too. The ride ain't easy, but take it as it is.

Weasel
systmaticwzl@gmail.com

to A. - i will never not love you.
   i've said what i had to say.

      to J. - love you, goof.

CUT THE LOSS

the sound inside

never danced among his waters
never smiled among his tears
trickling down our footsteps totter
stairs between his stars

you split my heart
right from the start
you catch
as i'm falling
down shores
afraid

but you're here
whispering
in my

ear

THE MUSES

allen ginsberg meditates while i eat breakfast

i ask him to stop chanting

low hums of nirvana
never found
shake the walls
of my home

the dogs
are somehow okay
with this

like some ride
on a dirt-road
they huddle
against the ground

when coffee spills
i ask him *what good
is enlightenment
when you've
never felt fulfilled*

he says *the soul
is always fulfilled
it's just the body
that's broken*

*unable to feel
what connection is lost
amidst all its nerves*

it seeks forgiveness

*but should
look for desire*

*break one heart
and you've done nothing
he says*

*we are all love
under dissatisfaction
our souls are sunflowers
waiting to sprout
waiting for madness*

hunter s. thompson aims his pistol at me

both hands
on the trigger

stance wide
in my hallway

he says the beer
in my fridge
is shit

when he tries to shoot
i ask him, *why haunt
a house with shit beer?*

fleshy stink weasel,
he says while adjusting
*the sun glasses resting
on his pale, cold face,*
i've been everywhere

i am frustrated
with sleeping
to the noise
of dissatisfaction

*spineless devil
where haven't
you been?*

his gun lowers
while hallway lights
dance panic

8

between us

in the pages of your books

the dead often look
distraught when
they're angry

i look him in the barrel
and tell him
*the devil has little
sympathy for the muses*

bukowski's ghost watches me fuck from the corner

while smoking a cigarette
his body sits tired
eyes squinted

he says i am not drunk enough
that being sober while fucking
is a delusion

i tell him in death
he is drunk enough
for us both

when i kiss the curve of your neck
he asks if the fires of madness
are worth the prayer to lessen our pain

i tell him
while stroking your cock
that there is only soul
in this room

the universe blessed me
when i tasted you

bukowski lights another cigarette
and grunts in the darkness

he says the world is waiting outside
and i tell him to let it wait
they'll still be pissed in the morning

i used a ouija board to talk to kerouac

he finally answered
after the eleventh call
typical writer, appearing
when he chose best

kerouac loved jazz
played a few notes
as his spirit pushed my fingers

this board was his typewriter
i, his transcription artist

he told me of all his lovers
that you still love in the afterlife

it only hurts more when the one
you're after travels away from you
and your left with the tiniest speck
of their body in the distance as a final memory

'cause you don't know if you'll see them
on the road when you're dead

as in life, it's just one giant road
everything in front
and all that's left behind
forgotten

kerouac blows out the candles
letting in the moonlight
taking another fit of whiskey

he says death don't matter
like life, it's only a dream

there's just another waiting
when you wake

hubert selby jr. drinks coffee in my kitchen

he smokes a cigarette
while the storm
settles in

the coffee is cold
but what's left to feel
when you're dead

*i was dying before
i was born*

the power flickers between us
texas weather ain't the nicest
when it's angry

i said, *we all know
death waits for us
somewhere*

he waived his hand
dismissive

lights another cigarette
the cloud leaving his lungs
dances in humid air

*life is a dream
fading*

*that is our requiem
an endeavor
we'll never hear*

*we all seek death
because there's never
any time to mourn
over our mistakes*

i talk in broken tongues

ain't a damn thing
to fix it

words shuffle
through cracked teeth
and tired lips

Some days all they do
is hang at the edge
tilting toward infinity
not ready to fall

ain't always a easy way to mend dirt
stuck in the cavern of my throat

but it don't matter

broken tongues still talk

love is not a synonym for monogamy

you're not playing
inside flames
by opening yourself

when i fell in love
outside of my marriage
i knew connection
was not singular

we all have
pieces inside
that simply can't
be put together
in one love alone

it is okay
to want to be
fulfilled
by giving up
yourself

when i was told me
i'd be jamming
forks in outlets

i said let the shocks happen
a good jolt doesn't kill you
it just makes you whole

my notebook is falling apart

it can't keep it together
for the both of us

glue dissolves
each time my fingers
peel back its pages

our spines are coming undone
stumbling into wrong days
getting tired of carrying
boulders as if i asked
for the tension

these pages are
as worn
as my lungs
choked from smoke
and dreams
of survival
long past

i never intended on lasting this long
my notebook knows this

has felt every gash
i've made
and every fit
of polished anger
steaming off
my bones

and if i ain't made

20

enough bad choices

my notebook is ready to retire
but i keep on saddlin' up

depression devours me from the inside

*all you have to do
is smile to feel better*

but how
do you move
your face without
hooking your
cheeks wide

listen to happier music

the notes
are weightless
saying nothing
except that
i am wrong
to feel this way

my teeth
are falling
from the cavern
of my jaw

nerves dead
from feeling pain
all too much

i've burned my hand
on the stove
so many times
the burn started
to feel normal

i can't just think happy

there is weight inside
my empty belly
and i can't find
where to cut first
to get it out

the wife/the faggot

when i was six years old
i had a friend
they called him trouble(d)
depending on the day

we played sega at his house
his mom hated mortal kombat
'cause of the blood that splattered
each time we landed a punch

one day
he led me to his room
power ranger toys spilled
on the floor
as if rita finally kicked
all their asses

he pulled on my arm
led me to his closet

the feeling of claustrophobia
at six years old
is like being in the center
of a riot

you just want out

he pushed me against the wall
i remember his clothes
hung like bodies on their hangers

his hand grabbed my crotch

called me his wife
and starts to undress me

then his mom found us

i remember thinking i was saved
light spiraling through darkness
as the door flushed open

i remember stumbling to put myself together
as if my legs could only work
with clothes

and before i could say anything
she called my mom
to pick me up

said, she knew I'd
always been a faggot

he says he knows why i smoke

that he has as many suicide notes
as i do cigarette packs

that the brain
in my skull
just needs the right air
to pull out toxins

doesn't he know
that weeds grow back

don't tell me i'm having
a bad day
some weeks i keep them
folded in my pocket

until i'm ready to feel
something other
than just
numb

i stopped looking
for poison ivy
in my body

there's not a drill
strong enough
to blast open
my skull

so when the urge
to puff itches

my skin

i light the fuck up

i want to tell him
i am addicted
to keeping calm
when panic tries
to break my bones

that i am waiting
for the end of my ride
as if life will be so
fucking merciful

but how do you dance
on lines of truth
without entangling
your feet in the crossfire
of judgment

i fuckin' hate knowin' a storm is comin'

waitin' for it to hit
feelin' winds pick up
unraveling with ease
as it saunters in uninvited

the unexpected traveler
arriving to fuck you up
leaving when it finishes
a final punch to your jaw

i walk my dog
in the front lawn
street painted dark
the earth's breath growing vile
before rain settles in

the neighbor's kids howl up the street
their voices carried between
shaking trees and stumbling branches

when the dog runs to the porch
my bones grow rigid

nature don't waste no time
when its pissed off
and sunrise seems too far
to wait on
when you're tired

i met apollo at a crossroad in texas

only sky ahead of me
he says, *no matter
where you turn,
it all ends
the same*

but all wolves tell you
what you already know

tell me what i don't know
instead of feeding me
a truth we all feel in our gut

your light is dimming
even at night your prophecy
holds weak between you and i

punch me in the chest
tell me how many potholes
i'm gonna fall into
on each side

so i can fall hard
so i can see hades
laugh at my broken ankles

you gods know everything

god of truth
tell me this

what happens at the end

of your story

you know mine all too well
and spoon feeding me
the last chapter
gets annoying

apollo

pinnacle of light
what will you do
when you fade out

the art of attachment

just when i think
I've written
all i could
ever write
your image
saunters in
uninvited

like a seance
of bad choices
you light
the candles
at midnight
to remind me
that we
happened

to remind me
that we
walked upward
in the snow
to share coffee

and that horror movies
with vampires scare
the ever-living
shit out of you

we cut the loss
years ago

loosened the balloon strings

attached to our sides
and let the sky
drift us apart

it is a practice
to let go

tell my why
you showed up now
when loving you
is an impossibility

the coffee at ihop sucks

i sit next to a window
to watch streetlights
and an empty parking lot

cars start to pack the freeway
as he pours watery sludge
into a mug

ain't no moon out tonight, he says
setting down the menu

i take a sip of weak caffeinated offerings
and admire the tattoo of bambi on his left wrist

i tell him, *even the moon needs rest*
it just steals from us
when it needs to

i met him in the woods for a quick blow-n-go

clouds lie overhead
wearing ash—business as usual
waiting to unleash the rains
they've carried for miles

he starts to unzip my jeans
calls me baby
but the word is foreign
like he's never called anyone baby
but enjoyed the thought

his flesh is stretched over his bones
easing outward as he slides
my pants to the grass

before he exposes my cock
to the warm, whispery air
a stench emerges around us

my head twists
eyes closing in confusion

when i realize he shit himself
i pull my clothes together
leave him with the trees

searching

for clean air

i have trouble staying in the present

i keep reaching for the end
cause there ain't no manual
on how to be human

like a book
i want to finish so fast
i tempt fate
to view the final page

it ain't easy
shufflin' feet on gravel
as if the ground
is constantly dancin'
jitterbug

constantly fearin' it'll split
because the panic button
won't shut off

panic is another word for numb
another word for turn everything off
'cause there's only so much

shouldering the weight of your expectations
versus the weight of wanting

to just
be
present

i run fast on empty
meditate to find the next world

only to see the devil
with clear skies

and he knows the weight
of my heart is splintering
slicing the inside of my chest

i asked him once
when he'd take me

he said, *i don't take fools
who remain unconscious*

the fire burns fierce this morning

sitting in traffic
while kicking flames
into my skull

as if my eyes are dull
and need more light
than the sun can give

it ain't easy
watching yourself
die every time
you close your eyes

but how do you meditate
past the feeling
of jumping off the cliff

of learning to grow weightless
to keep from reaching
the flat canvas waiting
for the entrails of your body
when you land

we trek along the beltway
slower than a rabbit
with its foot cut off

some mornings all i do is crawl
'cause my body can't think
to walk straight

i keep forgetting to breathe

as if taking in all the air
will keep the burns
on my flesh
from hurting

the process of healing is hardest
when your hands hold a grenade
waiting to blow the next
fit of rage into your bones

my bones know the embers
of anger all too well
prepared to break
upon impact

and before the final tick
before panic rides in
with its gang of bandits
ready to steal the remaining
fuel my body is running on

we move ahead
and the fires soothe
until the next time

the gas station of dull disdain

he holds the door open
a walking stick
arms as thick
as newborn branches

a quick thanks
drops from
my tongue

and when
i meet
his eyes
i see embers
of disgust

i've been down
this before

keep my head
forward

acknowledge
nobody

ain't no one
there to be
your friend

get out
dodge
before they
get stupid

i set a monster
on the counter

throw a couple
of bucks
while the cashier
yells at an employee
calling in sick

when he takes my cash
he mouths the words
get out
not safe

i stare back
at the dying tree
filling his cup
with ice

and as i jog
towards the door
i hear him

in burst of
dull disdain
the words
shoot from
his throat

bad enough you're a spic
had to be a fag too

II

For A

WHEN YOU SET SIGHT
UPON THE SKY
AT NIGHT

KEEP YOUR EYES OPEN

STARS ARE
SILENT
PRAYERS

GUIDING US
AS WE

DRIFT

when i heard you turned wishes into bombs

i took a quarter
and tossed it into
your well

your chest opened
ready to hold onto
the offering

and before the fireworks popped
i wished for the loudest
bang my ears ever heard

the first night

our bed was empty
i couldn't sleep

i kept thinking
you would crawl in
next to me

but i only felt
remnants of you

i thought i heard your breath
underneath the whirl of the fan

but you were gone
and i would have to wait
for you to return

when we got married

i pulled my heart
outta my back pocket
like it was my homework

wrinkled
worn
torn at the edges

little fox
it was just you
me, and the judge
but the room
never felt so alive

we didn't have rings
but we didn't care
clutching the paper
that sealed us tight

we're blind pilots
you and i
steering turbulent
while staying present

i just wanted to see
the art behind your smile

so i traced the staircase
of your spine
all the way up
to your neck

walked in time
to the thunder
beneath your chest

sunrise distant
but i'll be goddamned
if it didn't all dissolve
when i made it
to the top

i paint disasters when you're not around

i'm left counting dust
on the ceiling

a/c seems quieter
roaches—louder

little fox
this room holds
years of our
battles

years of rocks
flung at each other's face

like purgatory
it carries every
razor wired
note screamed
in fragile moments

i am attached
to your blades
meant to slice
frail flesh

it ain't so easy
reconciling
wounds that seem
to break open at will

but i'm learning

love ain't no fuckin' mercy

i forget where
we were
when you buried
your hatchet
in my chest

little fox
keep time on me
'cause i
lose track
of myself
way too often

sometimes
when your winds
are fierce
and hail spits
from your tongue
i think
of what
it'd be
like
to grow
weightless

but selling
our ghosts
won't do
no damn
good

moments

of fray
often
unravel

with
care

i return to you, love

at the airport
i text you when i board

and when you say
i love you

i feel as if i'm submerged in salt
as if fierce howls
of decadence await me
when i land

bukowski once said
love is a dog from hell

i wonder if he knew the pains
of bricks smashing your legs
or the upkeep of healing
wounds too far deep

love ain't no dog
but the hell it brings
is a side effect

when i tell you i love you
i hope the gash is light

and that the seeds
sprout trees
rather than
leaves

i could see the anger bubble in your belly

you plucked words like apples
spat them off your tongue
unable to keep them
in your throat

rage oozed up through your chest
you sat there like a dormant volcano
ready to erupt after years of slumber

little fox
i know the art
of growing numb
when it's all
you have
to keep you safe

when you told me to kill myself
i went home to safety
made my bed inside numbness
left walls unstained
ready to splinter
should i need to remember
what awaits outside

i know the taste
of scars unhealed

like raw, spoiled meat
it spreads across your tongue
until you've had enough

you never forget it

some days love is a wound
left open too long
weakening
scab chipping off

i still wish i knew
what was left
when i told you i tried

you are scrubbing the scuff-marks off the wall

telling me you'll keep your anger in check
that you'll do better

and i've heard this story before

soap drizzles down
i remember when

you made that mark
of how the rage shifted
to your hands

you ripped open a shoe box
threw it against the wall
and when the shaw of silence
entangled us both
you told me
i didn't calm you down
that i didn't soothe you
as a lover should

i said i'd get better
at building steeples
of devotion

i see you wash the stained walls
and i wonder how much of it
was my fault

thinking on all the love
you said i never gave you

of how my spine disappeared
and you were left with
a mold of numbness

how could you shape
anything from that?

i am worn
little fox

thin-skinned
and battle-scarred

and somewhere
in the core of my belly
i fear the new marks
yet to be made
on our walls

i don't get drunk

the smell makes me nauseous
you open the bottle of whiskey
pour down a few glasses
and go to town

my hands get nervous
fidgeting as i watch
sobriety leave your body

you tell me i lower you
that i treat you as a boy toy
while my other boyfriends
are held above you
painting a picture
of how little you mean
in my life

you laugh
and i can't tell
if you're joking

you tell me
i should fix my hair up
more often
as you run your fingers
through it

the smell of liquor
punches me back
and i want to vomit

i am good at holding

myself together
in times of awkward
encounters

when you get bored
you pour yourself another
while i head to bed

i never wanted to write our break-up poem

but the river between us
is overflowing
little fox

i have pushed through
the currents of your rage
beaten down by the hail
of your teeth

and i'm growing weak

exhaustion engraved
in my shoulders

i have stopped seeing
what lies beyond
the smog of ourselves

i've learned the art
of getting your
hands dirty

of working
on being whole
only to find
that perfection
is a death rattle

i love you
but how far
can love go
when you're

unable to breathe

unable to feel loved
when you've been
made to feel inhuman

little fox
you are a firecracker
in the heat of june
and i kept touchin'
your flames
'cause gettin'
burned by you
was magic

i heard the word love
and i thought of you

but love is wound
that needs care
and i have grown
infected over the years

i dropped him off at the greyhound

boy wrapped
in a grown
man's body

i parked the car
on the side
while a couple
homeless dudes
ran naked
in the street

i grabbed his bags
waters rushing
down our cheeks

my fingers didn't want
to let go of the eons
we created

but if my grip
stayed tight
we would be lost
among pleiades
navigating stars
without growing

our journey long over
when he got on his bus
i collapsed in the car

begging atlas
carrier of the heavens

60

grant me a compass
to navigate the rivers
of our departure

the future is another ditch, beginning at dirt

there's so much
time to think
yet nothing
to say

like knives
words grow dull
the more you
throw them

you asked me
to see what
we are

i told you
we were
a temple

c o l l a p s i n g

bricks shuffling
out of place

you wiped rust
from your eyes
said we could
start anew

we have
been reborn
little fox

but old habits
never die young

you said i just
need sleep
but i tire
of putting
trust in dreams
to fix the decay
spreading
between us

i took your spot on the bed

you always complained
that the mattress
was too busted

i gave you
the firmer
side

as i slept
in the void

sinking
without
support from
the frame

when you left
i slept in my grief

continued to dive
down before sleep
settled over my bones

but tonight there's a new moon
a hole in the sky
and the waves
of decay
stop

i put on some
new sheets
stop looking

64
for you
when light
goes out

like a vinyl skip
to a different
day

a house of broken ghosts

they always haunt me
at the worst moments

screeching hollow
at midnight
as if spitting confetti
will make living
any easier

i want them to slow down
take their time
but they only know bedlam

slamming pots against the walls
to a song of their own rhythm

i tell them i just want to sleep
that i have written their cluttered
lyrics on my arms as a cease fire

my skull unraveling at the stitches
like a costume sewed to flesh

they tell me that swallowing doom
is like swallowing pills
it goes down hard at first
but you get used to it
with time

the clown sits on my wall

black holes in his skull
fixated at his reflection

searching for the past
hiding underneath the paint—
a moment he needed to let go

he and i are both alike
piling forged smiles
over scars and cigarette burns

waiting
for a way
out

i wrote my suicide note on a napkin

it says it wasn't your fault
that i got no demons
only weights
pushing me further
into the soil

when the universe wants you
to return
it pulls hard
and i have danced
its number more
than i care to
remember

exhaustion is only
entangled in my spirit

don't feed me coins
death will have
to take me broke

when it calls
you only see the world
through a kaleidoscope
and my sight has not
yet recovered

my note says i love you
i love you more than
the wind's breath before a storm

but i tire of living

with the crisis
that is myself

i have tasted
the words
of rain waters

swam in floods
created from
hurricanes

yet the art of breathing
when submerged
is beyond the reach of my
broken arms

my note says
don't pray for me

there's still
miles to swim
after death

i ain't no prayin' man

the air is
still tonight

a dog howls
in the silence

and i wonder
if death
has come
to meet me

i've never
had a stalker
approach me
in person

i tire of reachin'
for amethysts
when my fingers
grab ashes

the stars are all on their smoke break
i wait for rest to overtake me
not afraid of death
exhausted with living

i have yet to fill
the graveyard of bad choices
i've worked hard to create

i light a cigarette
disappointed

in being alone tonight

but when i finally sleep
vutures will swirl overhead
to get a piece of what
i've left behind

afterglow on a desk stained with coffee

he tells me, *i ain't killed myself yet*
as if to say light is a small death
he wants to caress

but we can't touch flames
only embers
when we're tired

of seeing the sun set
in the morning

morning coffee at the gas station

i get it
up the road
on weekends

five-minute drive
it's the only time
i don't smoke

thunder meanders
in morning clouds
as i park

he sits at the door
tells me to take a seat
once i've gotten my fuel

knows my routine
all too well

older man
the heart tattoo
on his hand
makes him
mildly cute

while i poured
liquid sludge
into a cheap cup

i imagined us
in the bathroom
for a morning quickie

when i sat at his park bench
he starts to shuffle
then lays out a tarot card

the empress
reversed

his hands were worn
dry skin peeling
from his palms

twitching his fingers together
he let out a large sigh

said my card tells me
i'm unfulfilled
that i have been dependent
on bad weather scars—a warning

i tell him, *though the coffee
is still hot, it cools easily,
i've got a few years
to create new ones*

he asked me to eat his ass

i was all too willing
to oblige

spreading his cheeks wide
as if opening a bag
of groceries

my thumbs play with his hole
he lets out a quiet moan
only audible to the choir
of silence in this room

i draw his ass closer
my tongue ready
to plunge

but the moment
i get inches away
it hits me

rotten
like a bad
caesar salad
left out
in texas heat

boy

do you not know
the basics of washing
your ass?

you can't
present
a feast
that's
rotten

what do you tell
your guests
when they are
not able
to cure
their desire

i pushed him off
said i felt sick

a small piece
of toilet paper
lies on my belly

i fling it away
grabbed my clothes
and didn't call
the next day

the boss lost to the carnage of a drunk driver

i ain't the sort
to put weight
in dreams

but i remember
how charcoal
blanketed the sky

a thin fog loitering
between my co-workers
all dressed in grief

voices cut
from our throat

we stood encircled
in a heaviness
unknown

there was a piece
missing in
the office

a bone dissolved
that kept us tight

i awoke to the news
the next morning

hipnos

beneath this texas sky
clouds shape the wings
of your head

mosquitoes swarm
aching to taste
my blood this evening
marking their territory
along my arms

i have run my body ragged
made sleep an afterthought
in hopes my dreams
will hold better omens

what seeds have you brought
god of sleep

will they quiet the flames
loitering in the air

or am i destined
to hold insomnia close
like a lover i can't let go

everytime i call

walls bounce
with her
laughter

while her
dogs shout
thunder
claps
in the
hallway

i pull the phone'
from my ear
and let
the echoes

pour
out

IV

For J

I DONT NEED
THE STARS
TO SEE YOUR
PERFECTION

PLEIADES BE DAMNED

I'LL SEE YOU
AT THE BEND
OF YOUR

SMILE

the grogginess of your voice

slithers through my skull
every morning
before coffee brews
before the first drag
of smoke enters my lungs

i keep the phone pressed to my ear
sun still hiding beneath
a misshaped moon

when your roots
unfurled
i plucked them
like heartstrings

i couldn't let go
of your pulse

i like that you call me star

that you stick your hand
in the fog of my body
and make me feel human

there are too many weeds
circling the stitches
i've lived off of

lover

i am terrible at gardening
bullet wounds
made from past experience

learning how to live
while carrying the weight
of armageddon

yet you dive in
head first
still finding
some spire of beauty
to keep me conscious

my tongue longs for the taste of you

airport deserted
my tongue longs
for the taste
of ash
as i step off
the plane

heart ticking—
raging

for a breath
of heat
and smoke
to soothe
its fixation

before i bring the stick
to my lips

i see you

and all
i want
is

you

i never understood the appeal of fucking in a shower

until i met you

water poured
over us
as you leaned
against the wall

my hands moved
from your sides
to your hips
as i thrust
against your body

your moan
rose beneath
the noise of pipes
and steam

i followed
your breath
hands
clenched

you made me ravenous
eager to satiate my desire
my hips moved faster

and when i felt that
jolt of ecstasy
shoot through my bones

i held on tighter

breathless
under the steam
and dying water

i think about your touch on the coldest nights

rain taps the window
as you curl your fingers
across my chest

i kiss your cheek
and the wind moves
silently outside

adonis

you have given me
something
i've never had
before

stung my heart
like a wasp
and left your mark
on a landscape
underprepared
for love

when you nuzzled into me
i didn't want to let go
i just wanted to get lost
on the sea of your skin
and stare at the open moon
sky devoid of stars

but stars only help
if you need to find
the shore

and i'm not ready
to return to land
just yet

it's been months since i've seen you

yet i still remember
the smooth form
of your body
pressed to mine

your taste has spoiled my tongue
creating a drought
i am all too eager
to cure

lover

it ain't easy sittin'
miles away
thinkin'
of next
time

patience is only
so strong
when stretched far
in between

but when my plane lands
i'll know i've left
the walls of limbo
behind

you wear me out

like the time we played dodgeball
on a trampoline
and all i could see
was this big-ass smile
on your face before my throw
missed your body

my aim was never that great

you started climbing
the obstacle course
and all i could do was fall
but it didn't matter

my lungs were giving
out by the time you finished
and i laughed because i never swam
on padded flooring before

i still think you let me win
at one-on-one combat

gravity ain't my best friend

but when you fell into a pool
of ketchup colored squares
i could only think of how
the divine falls with grace

i never thought it'd be cold in april

sun peeks through
the tapestry

surrounded
by icy
air
i roll
to my back

quaking

lungs exhale
a large bite
of breath
and before
i could
find the
cover

you roll into me
sleeping
still

i wrap
an arm
around
you

it's not
so cold
anymore

i've never been blown in a graveyard
(to the dead who saw)

you pull me behind a tree
as dusk settles in
lips entangled

i see them

old timers
spirits without
shit to do

when your lips
wrap hard
around
my shaft
i see
nobody
but i know eyes
watch in the
distance

lover

don't you know
ghosts love excitement?

cold air whips my ass
as you finish

pulling me together
as dark rides in

94
    the dead can't see everything
    but as we leave
    i see them
    gather

    hungrier than i am
    to finish the night

love is a gospel, and i'm still learning

i am rigid
tattered edges shape my core
yet all you see
is perfection

my body is stitched up
one too many times

it is what
you make
of it

you still trail your hand
along my belly
as if the thread
was never there

lover

i don't know
the art of being wanted

night still full
contrarian

i am tired of apologizing
for existing
yet you know this
somehow
like you're tuned
in to the anxiety
etched in my bones

go slow babe
i'm still new at this

my skull is a choir
of broken ghosts
and you silence
all of them
when you plant
that hickie on my neck
and call me

Adonis

your heart is just the chatter of your body

though you
are farther
than the sun
on most days

my hands still
feel the curve
of your hips

or how your neck
bends when you
tilt your head

love is
madness
hitting all
the right
spots in
our
bodies

lover

grab your pen
empty as it is
fill it with
each beat

shooting straight
is impossible
when delirium
enters our

triggers

pull words
from your
bones

poets only know
what fires
lie inside

i drove with aphrodite on i-10

kesha blares through speakers
as the sky stays dull

stars retired
i lie back
and wonder
why the moon
continues
to split apart

we had been driving
for what seemed
like eternity

but you wouldn't
let go of my hand

lover

driving one-handed
is a skill best
learned with certainty

i brush your arm
the weight of exhaustion
covering me
like a blanket

and when i tell you
i want to live
with you

100
    you say to bring it on
    that this long haul
    is worth every
    drop of rain
    from the pale
    black sky

the first time you get blown at disney

people scream
as the tower
of terror plummets
to madness

you tell me
to come
to the last
stall

knock

be
quiet

mick ain't
got time
for quickies
in his town

i enter amidst
wailing children

aerosmith invades
the park, soft
guitar strings
blending in crowds

you waste
nothing

yanking me close

for a kiss before
sliding my cock
into your mouth

muffled breaths
are hushed
by stomping
footsteps
as you take
me whole

lover

i have never
allowed sweet emotion
to jam while venturing
into uncharted eroticism

but i'll walk
on your bad side

downpours heavy
i am all too eager
to follow you
through waterfalls
and uncertainty

comfort is another
word for lifeless
and you are all
too full of vigor

and as we finish
this carnal roller-coaster

you pull me together

leading me to another
impulsive endangerment

you always had
a sense of adventure

eros makes reservations
(*for our anniversary*)

it started raining
when we hit
the road

traffic—an endless endeavor

to a guy who views
the olive garden
as a nice restaurant

hearing the word reservations
tipped the boat
floating in my skull

my brain flooded
with whatever stars
it could grab to piece
together the surprise

it wasn't an image
i could bring to light

i learned to take the ride
not every destination
needs to be known

the unknown ain't
so damn scary
when you're with
the adventurous

we almost didn't make it
rain gushed over our car
as we parked across

i still couldn't figure it out
but when we entered
this cave of quixotic
romanticism

my heart stopped

lover

i will never know
how you keep
surprising me
with wild endeavors

nude portraits on the walls
they sat us at a table
blending dessert
and passion

when they wrote
happy anniversary
in chocolate

i fell harder in love
a new feeling
bubbling from
my skin

as if all my past lovers
spoke weak maudlin

while remaining
just uncaring enough

you never told me
you were eros

as we dried off
with coffee
i couldn't stop
dreaming of the next
chapter we decided
to venture into

a past fragmented
(in response to "The State of His House" by Thurston Howl)

being terrified
is an understatement
when you live
in a home
so brittle

you call it
a past
fragmented

the walls
hold every
bruise
laid bare
before them

some scars are
too wounded
to be shown

lined with salt
around the edges
waiting for
the wrong
touch

lover

my house
is a collection
of ghosts

when you say
you want to
"beat out the
rust from
the gears
of both
our pasts"

i want to
get to work

a wrench ain't enough
but you can grab
anything in my
garden of broken tools

this waltzing panic
has fumed so long
and want nothing more
than to cut out the
earthquake that's
been rattling
for years

our house will
have its cracks
and its stains

but it won't
have the broken
ghosts hitching
on our backs

only us

punk rock taught me that life is a moment

fuck playin' safe
toss your body
in the pit
because the sun
will rise whether
you see it
or not

let yourself fall
the scrape
is just a lesson
to fall again

moon stomping
is a dance best
learned with broken feet

keep learning
to fall well
and take
everything
with calm

because your heart
is a grenade
pin ripped out
ticking
for the next
riot

the ghost in my house keeps throwing dildos at me

it's irritating getting up to take a piss
only to get hit with a silicone penis

it likes to make sure
i get hit with the knot
as if the thickest part
of the shaft would make
me aim better
in the dim lighting
of my bathroom

the roaches find it funny
hiding in the corners
as this specter arms itself
with another sexual fantasy
encased in an expensive toy

the mouse watches from the shelf
enjoying the impact; satisfactory revenge
for me murdering its family last winter

the dog doesn't seem to be concerned
he watches from the doorway
wondering when his food bowl
will be refilled

i asked it what it wanted
using the last of my lube
it wrote a message on the sheets

it said it couldn't find
a clean knife

to throw at me
that it settled
for the next best item
only wishing it were sharper

my dating profile

my name is weasel
don't ask me how i got the name
or what's my real name
it ain't your business
til i tell you

i got good days
and bad days
and most times
i don't know
which is which

i just take it
as it comes
like a fluctuating
Paycheck

lotta times
it's on the low end

i got 2 dreams
be an academic professor
and own a taco truck

my boyfriend
love him to death
but i know he cringes
at the thought of me
dreaming of tacos

what he doesn't know
is that when i have my mid-life crisis

i ain't gettin a motorcycle

My dog's named buddy
he clutches to
my husband's pillow
like i still clutch his name
on my weak nights

he left a few days back
i'm still adjusting
to having so much
space in a tiny home

recovering from an unstable
relationship ain't easy
and most days i just want
to throw the hurricane back
in my life and tell myself
it'll get better

i ain't so good at recognizing my emotions
but i write poems to process
through how numb my body
can become

i'm wrong a lot of times
but when i'm right
you best believe
i'm gonna own that shit
til it becomes socially awkward

i'm dtf but don't call me daddy

i don't love the outdoors

nature and me don't get along
and every guy i meet
wants to play pan's flute
and bang under a tree
cause it's "romantic"

when mosquitoes
bite your ass
it ain't romantic

i've smashed heads
at judas priest shows
and i know more about
the pits than anyone
under 30

don't tell me my age
it's just a time bomb
and i ain't ready for it
to blow

we all know goofy fucks

but i wonder
what that dopey
bastard
gets off to

i bet he opts
for the handcuffs
when he waltz
into romance & more

hyucking his way
through the vibrators
and garterbelts
latching onto
a harness he'd
been saving up for
'cause disney
don't pay shit

when he takes
someone to his bed
does he beg to be
the "good boy"

or desire his thighs
to be pummeled
sniveling beneath
a gag fitted for his mouth

goofy walks into a club

he likes to get fucked up
do shots out of
twink boy asses

tired of letting the old mouse
ride his dick after hours
he twerks on the dance floor

foxy flare saunters up
to the old dog
cock out
ready to mingle

when his ass starts to hurt
he hyucks his way off to the bar
but the fox catches his harness

the two lock eyes
music screaming
the sky is falling
the fox drops
and massages the dogs
old cock

not ready to retire yet
he does another shot
and lets his new partner
take the wheel

pan's flute plays in disarray

is this how you consume
your loneliness?

god of who the fuck knows
luring hungry lovers
to satiate your appetite

you've got a sharp desire
drawing me to the woods
notes of your flute
playing circles
in the air

keep playing
i don't hold indiscretions
like dominoes

your notes pierce
my belly like a blade
and i am all too eager
to fill your ravenous
intentions

your body is lighter
than a collection
of feathers

when i touch you
i can feel your heart
screaming to be
devoured

let's skip past the seduction
your sexual powers
are as disillusioned
as your past lovers

i know when we finish this game
you'll have disappeared

leaving me
with nothing
but a chip
of your horn

i met satan on grindr

who needs to sign
your fuckin' book
when all i wanna do
is fuck you over
your flames

stand tall over me
defiler of souls
my body is devoid
of christian doctrine

souls are aimless
the heart is what
drives the body
to desire

what is it you really want
lie down upon your
sacrificial rock

spread yourself open
scratch your symbol
on my back
as i enter your cavern

i've danced the tango
with evil enough times
to know the game
is short but memorable

and when we're finished
keep my number

i may need to know
what death feels like
after a few more orgasms

everyone is so afraid of demons

but i'd fuck baphomet
in a frightened minute

i mean, i may want dinner first
seein' as he's an almighty being
of evil and death
(according to the christians)

but if that lil goat devil
approached me
i'd open up my bed

possess me in ways
i ain't never heard of

set the booze down
i want to be sober
when i see your throne

when i warm it up
take the ride
evil is a mutual endeavor

i'll get lost in your horns
curving from your head

fuck the baptism by fire
who needs heat
when you're already sanctified

the americana

she does the sign
of the cross
when i mention
the thickness
of a dildo

johnny cash hangs
on the wall

i'm not so sure
he approved of my
sexual encounter
with pan

but i didn't feel
no ring of fire
blazin' beneath me

when i finished
the preacher man
was all too eager
to pluck his banjo

wanted to get jesus
back in the bar
before i conjured
another spirit
with a ouija board

on my drive home
i wondered
if i'd be let back

on the stage
for another round

or if they re-blessed
the tables
when i left

compassion is often rough

when my first dog died
i was made to dress
like a minion at work

never given time
to grieve, i sang
that stupid banana
song to get second place
at a halloween contest

buried in my back yard
i still try to tread light
over his patch of grass

the rattle never left his throat
hand on his chest
i wondered if he knew
i was there before taking off

when my second dog passed
i cradled him in my arms
kissed his forehead
before rest overcame him
the cancer had already taken
most of his body

i had to keep telling myself
mercy, was not always pretty
that compassion is a practice
we are far under-prepared for
goodbye is an attachment
that is tight around our fingers

i would give anything
to hug my boys again

but when you let go
you have to do it
with love

anything less
and you're
still holding on

when my lights go out

don't return me to the earth
my body is not one
for lying dormant

burn me on a bonfire
let my bones grow
brittle under the rage
of gasoline and flames

i want to drift
like kerouac

see nothing but empty roads
'cause i tire of the same sky
every day

my ashes will find a home
in the next life
amongst broken cadillacs
ridden past their expiration date

still finding saddened tongues
and un-tuned guitar strings

maybe then
i'll finally know
what it means
to rest

exit

when the rain
steals from us another song
we play along
we sing along

when the sky
wraps around us
his skeleton bones
we sing along
we carry on

you stand there
at the edge of my doorstep
but i'm not there
my body's home
my mind is gone

somewhere

Other Titles by the Author

Poetry
Born Into This
a warm place to self-destruct
we don't make it out alive

Fiction
Cigarette Burns
We Live for Half-Moons
Jazz at the End of the Night

Films
Poetry is Dead

CD
a warm place to self-destruct

Edited by the Author
Degenerates: Voices for Peace
DREAD: A furry horror mag
Furnicate
The Haunted Traveler
How Well You Walk through Madness
Knotted
Ordinary Madness
Open Mind
Passing Through
Purrgatorio
Typewriter Emergencies
Vagabonds: Anthology of the Mad Ones

WEASEL is a degenerate author and The Dude of Weasel Press. His work has appeared in anthologies such as *Slashers, Infurno, Sinister Sheets, Thirteen Poets, Five2One Magazine*. In 2016 he was a Juried Poet for the Houston Poetry Fest.

http://degenerateweasel.weebly.com

Acknowledgments

I'd like to extend a deepest thanks to the folks below:

Chris Wise, David E. Cowen, Z.M. Wise, Mary Margaret Carlisle, Ann Fogelman, Brian Kehinde, Ken Jones, Emily Ramser, Matthew David Campbell, Edward Viduarre, LuLynne Streeter, Neil S. Reddy, Carmen Jacobson--a strong collective of writers and kick ass friends. Thank you for supporting Weasel Press and our publishing endeavors.

Arronn, thank you. I'll always hold everything we shared close. We're on different paths. Keep moving forward, little fox.

Donna McClendon, who I'm sure we're gonna open up a damn liquor store one day. #knuckifyoubuck

Alex Garza, man, we fuckin' old. Thank you, bro. We gotta catch up again, I'll cook the fajitas like the old days.

BanWynn OakShadow, thanks for the idea on fucking Satan. Maybe I'll meet him someday.

JR, thank you.

Jonny, thank you, love. And don't ask "for what," 'cause I know, you know. Goober. Love you, bae.

Weasel Press is a publisher of bold poetry and fiction. Starting as Vagabonds: Anthology of the Mad Ones, a journal of modern beat works, Weasel Press has been publishing for seven years.

We're the renegades; opening a space for voices not often heard. Dedicated to quality literature and quality production, we house ourselves in Texas. Publishing up to 10 authors a year, we're a machine that keeps on going.

Grab a title. Learn more about us. Join the community we thrive on cultivating, or join the staff! Support your local indie publishers, authors, artists. This work is a communal effort.

To learn more go to www.weaselpress.com

Other Titles from Weasel Press

Pan's Saxophone by Jonel Abellanosa
Hyper-Real Reboots by Sudeep Adhikari
Wayward Realm by Sendokidu Adomi
Ghost Train by Matt Borczon
To Burn in Torturous Algorithms by Heath Brougher
Klonopin Meets Sisyphus by Adam Levon Brown
The House of Eros by Matthew David Campbell
Harmonious Anarchy by Matthew David Campbell
H A I L by Stanford Cheung
Still Life Over Coffee by Robert Cone
The Madness of Empty Spaces by David E. Cowen
The Seven Yards of Sorrow by David E. Cowen
Bleeding Saffron by David E. Cowen
Face Down in the Leaves by Dwale
Wine Country by Robin Wyatt Dunn
Smash & Grab Poems by Ryan Quinn Flanagan
In Winter's Dreams We Wake by Ryan Quinn Flanagan
If the Hero of Time was Black by Ashley Harris
Dormant Volcano by Ken Jones
Evergreen by Sarah Frances Moran
I Am A Terrorist by Sarah Frances Moran
I'll Only Write Poems for You by Max Mundan
Rising from the Ashes by Meghan O'Hern
Lipstick Stained Masculinity by Mason O'Hern
Chaos Songs by Scott Thomas Outlar
Kisses and Kickflips by Kacey Pinkerton
In Another Life, Maybe by Michael Prihoda
the first breath you take after giving up by Michael Prihoda
the same that happened yesterday by Michael Prihoda
Beneath this Planetarium by Michael Prihoda
Years without Room by Michael Prihoda
Toast is Just Bread that Put Up A Fight by Emily Ramser
I forgot How To Write When They Diagnosed Me by Emily Ramser
Conjuring Her by Emily Ramser
UHAUL: A Collection of Lesbian Love Poems by Emily Ramser
The Escape by Rayah

Taste & See by Neil S. Reddy
Inevitable by Amy L. Sasser
Satan's Sweethearts by Marge Simon and Mary Turzillo
Colliding with Orion by Chris Wise
Cuentos de Amor by Z.M. Wise
Wolf: An Epic and Other Poems by Z.M. Wise
Kosmish and the Horned Ones by Z.M. Wise
Ghostly Pornographers by Thomas White

www.ingramcontent.com/pod-product-compliance
Lightning Source LLC
Chambersburg PA
CBHW020936090426
42736CB00010B/1157